# KICKIN OFFICE LEASE

## 6 PROVEN STEPS
### TO DEVELOP A THOROUGH STRATEGY
### AND AVOID COSTLY MISTAKES

JON MILONAS

# ACKNOWLEDGEMENTS

Thank you to my family at The Strategic Coach, Inc., who encouraged me to write this book, especially Dan Sullivan, Babs Smith, Lee Brower and Maureen Sullivan. Thanks to Hill Hammock, who sat with me to sort out the early vision and outline. Thank you to my clients and mentors, who helped bring clarity to my thoughts and words and provided invaluable feedback along the way, specifically Eric Schoonveld, Mike Motyka, Jim Beavers, Jerry DiCola, Diana Hernandez, Anne Dysart Vergiels, Gaylene Domer, Sarrah Stutzman, Jeremy Gottschalk and Dan Walser. To Tom Ziegler, my editor, who provided much needed leadership throughout the process. Thank you to Victor Kore for carrying the marketing of the book over the finish line.

I wouldn't be in this industry had it not been for Mary Barrett, Jeff Barrett, Bill Novelli, Jeff Mann, George Kohl, Scott Brandwein, Jamie Georgas and Jack Durburg. Thank you for taking me under your wing and believing in me when I was 23 years old and I didn't know a single thing about commercial real estate. To my colleagues at CBRE, who push me to better serve our clients every day, and for your friendship, thank you. Thank you to my parents, Jim and Karen Milonas, for teaching me integrity, faith and hard work. To my amazing wife, Melissa, thank you for patiently and graciously encouraging me to pour countless hours into this book. Most importantly, I thank God for the joy of life.

# TABLE OF CONTENTS

Introduction                                          VII

**STEP 1**: What Are Your Deficiency Drivers?          1

**STEP 2**: What Are Your Success Factors?             9

**STEP 3**: What Are Your Scenarios?                  19

**STEP 4**: Who Is On Your Team?                      29

**STEP 5**: What Is Your Schedule?                    43

**STEP 6**: What Is Your Budget?                      59

Kicking Off Your Office Lease                         69

Appendix – Glossary of Key Terms                      73

# INTRODUCTION

I recently had lunch with the facilities director of a 125-person organization in Chicago. We met the week before at an event where I was speaking. After my presentation, she invited me to visit the new 25,000 square foot office she designed and constructed six months prior. It was fantastic! I could see the joy in her eyes as she walked me through the space, describing the different business groups, client-facing areas, design elements, furniture solutions, functionality of the new technology and much more.

Afterward, at lunch, I learned that this most recent office relocation was the fifth project she had executed at her company. She'd completed her first project 25 years earlier when there were only six employees and she was the executive assistant to the CEO. During her first project, she shared with me, she didn't have the slightest clue as to how to run an office leasing process. She learned through trial and error, but not without making many mistakes along the way.

Years after her first project, her company had grown to 125 employees, and she recognized communication within the office was severely lacking. She told her new CEO the business would benefit from greater transparency and they should consider moving to a more open plan where no one would have an office—including the CEO himself. To her surprise, he said, "OK, make it happen—but if it isn't a success, it's your job on the line!"

What had she gotten herself into? She had some experience from prior projects, but now she had to figure out the change management associated with pulling people out of their offices where they'd been for 20-plus years and putting them in cubes! And who knew—maybe her previous experience was more of a liability than an asset. What resources could she turn to? Scared to death, she made a beeline to the Borders on Michigan Avenue (this was back when people still went to bookstores) and began to read everything she could about office space as she started to formulate her plan. During her research she stumbled across a staggering statistic that 50 percent of people who manage a major office relocation project either get fired or quit!

Well, as you know, she didn't lose her job. In fact, she told me, the CEO was so thrilled with her efforts and the rave reviews she got once the project was completed, he gave her complete leadership over all the company's office projects in both Chicago and eight satellite offices across the country.

As we finished lunch, I told her about the book I wanted to write. Her response was immediate: "You have to finish writing it! I know firsthand what it's like to feel the tremendous pressure of pulling off an office leasing project, the fear of failing, the battles involved in gaining internal buy-in, the challenge of not disappointing my colleagues. An office lease is signed what—every three, five, ten years? Very few people actually know what they are doing. People like me—and there are so many of us—need your roadmap. If only I'd had a book like yours when I started 25 years ago!"

I can't tell you how much that resonated with me, because the need she was describing aligned so directly with the value I want to bring to you, the reader. This was just one of several conversations I was having, almost weekly, with very successful business leaders who had little to no experience managing an office leasing project—CEOs of tech startups, CFOs of marketing agencies, new Managing Partners or COOs of law firms, Executive Directors of nonprofits, board members of private equity firms, and new facility directors of large Fortune 500 corporations—most of their questions and concerns were the same.

So I sat down one day and outlined a very detailed, step-by-step process on how to run a real estate project from start to finish. I was determined to place every bit of knowledge I had into the pages of that book, and by the time I was done, I was staring at 30 pages of bullet points and notes—and that was just the outline! The actual book, I imagined, would end up being 300 pages long!

But when I asked a few mentors and clients if that was what they'd want to read, they said no, and the consensus was clear: Instead of a lengthy and wordy guide that tried to cover every aspect of the leasing journey, they suggested I write a concise guide to help <u>kick it off</u> and set the right direction and foundation for success, while avoiding very costly mistakes along the way.

Think about it: If you have the task of managing your office's leasing project, do you really need to be an expert on every detail of the process, from scouting new locations to plugging in that last phone? Getting caught up in all the less important priorities can outweigh the needs of your business, but if you can go into a project armed with a familiarity of the process and a strategy for building an advisory team around you, you'll be in much better shape, and you'll avoid a lot of heartache down the road.

My plan is to give you those building blocks and empower you to create a workable vision, strategy and roadmap for your future office lease. I want you to consider this book as a thinking exercise that helps organize your thoughts, opinions and questions. There are several pages at the end of the book for your notes and opportunities throughout the chapters to write your thoughts down as well. Whether you're the CEO of a 5,000-person company, you're opening your first small office for six people or you're the facilities director of a 125-person organization who's just been told her job is on the line, I will lead you through six proven Kick-Off Questions designed to get you going and kick off your process successfully.

Those six Kick-Off Questions are:

1. **What Are Your Deficiency Drivers?** Targeting the factors in your current office space and leasing situation that are not ideal and are holding your organization back.
2. **What Are Your Success Factors?** Envisioning what needs to happen during the course of your office leasing process to make it a huge success.
3. **What Are Your Scenarios?** Identifying the most likely real estate scenarios that match the needs of your organization.
4. **Who Is On Your Team?** Selecting the internal and external players you need to orchestrate a successful office leasing process.
5. **What Is Your Schedule?** Plotting your timeline to reach a successful outcome.
6. **What Is Your Budget?** Calculating the estimated financial projections that factor into your budget prior to kicking off your leasing project.

With that being said, let's jump right into Kick-Off Question One, which is 100 percent focused on you and your current situation.

# STEP 1

# *What Are Your Deficiency Drivers?*

*Targeting the factors in your current office space and leasing situation that are not ideal and are holding your organization back.*

There is often a tremendous gap between a company's office space and the way its business will function in the future. Businesses and industries change, but the space remains fixed. Over time, your growing organization has to make the best of facilities designed for a younger company as your new business units or practice groups squeeze into the existing space. As your organization changes, it may feel like you're trying to stuff 20 pounds of flour into a 10-pound sack.

## YOUR DEFICIENCY DRIVERS

What causes difficulties within your office space? I call them "Deficiency Drivers," and every company will face several of them during a business' life cycle.

Deficiency Drivers go beyond a simple problem like not having enough conference rooms. They speak to all the shortcomings that follow: Does your lack of conference rooms limit

1

your teams from collaborating in a way that sparks new solutions for your clients? Does it limit the number of clients and visitors who can come to your office, which stifles the growth of those relationships? Does it limit your use of new technologies to connect with colleagues or clients around the globe?

*Deficiency Drivers impact every part of your organization: culture, flexibility, communication, growth, mentorship, camaraderie, creativity, confidence, collaboration—and ultimately your bottom line.*

Of the hundreds of Deficiency Drivers based on client feedback I've gotten over the years, here are the top 10 along with their causes. You may not identify with all 10, but many of them will apply to your organization.

We're starting the process here because our ability to recognize what doesn't work gives our minds the opportunity to envision what would work. As you read through the list below, please check boxes next to the Deficiency Drivers that are limiting your organization's potential. If you're contemplating opening a new office, compare this list to your past experiences.

## 1. The space no longer fits your needs.

- ☐ The office design looks and feels old and stale, or it lacks warmth and vibrancy.
- ☐ There is little natural light.
- ☐ There are few places within the office for collaboration.
- ☐ The space does not impress clients or help in attracting new talent.
- ☐ Your business has progressed, transformed, grown up, adapted, succeeded and become more sophisticated, while the space has become stagnant, inefficient and even obsolete.

## 2. You're paying more rent than you should.

- ☐ A drop in company revenue has driven your leasing costs too high as a percentage of sales or annual budgets.
- ☐ A change in the market has adjusted rental rates down, and now you're paying too much by comparison.
- ☐ Rent escalations in your lease have drastically increased your rental rate over time, and toward the end of the lease, your rent is far too high.
- ☐ Your building has been redeveloped, sold, refinanced or upgraded, which has significantly increased your real estate taxes and operating expenses or your future rent if you choose to renegotiate and renew your lease.

## 3. Former leaders who once made the real estate decisions for your company have moved on, and the new leadership has a different vision for:

- ☐ The office location.
- ☐ Building quality.
- ☐ Design standards.
- ☐ Office layout.
- ☐ Cost.
- ☐ Recruitment and retention.

## 4. You have too little space. (This is a great problem to have!)

- ☐ Your company may be bursting at the seams, creating a need to expand sooner than you'd anticipated.
- ☐ Your company may be functioning short term in temporary space prior to establishing a longer-term office in a specific market.
- ☐ There are enough seats for employees, but a lack of other shared spaces (café, conference rooms, training rooms, etc.).

### 5. You have too much space.

- ☐ Part of your company was sold, or there were layoffs, leaving excess area.
- ☐ Your company intentionally did not backfill positions as employees retired, quit, moved, etc.
- ☐ Your business model changed, which requires a different number of employees or a different skill set.
- ☐ More employees are telecommuting, travelling or working at client sites.
- ☐ You are able to do more with less space, and changes in the way you use furniture or technology have left parts of the office unused.

### 6. The space is not configured the right way.

- ☐ Reception is too large or small.
- ☐ Your offices are too large or small.
- ☐ You have too many conference rooms or not enough; they're the wrong size or not the right type; their technology is not adequate for teleconferencing, presentations, etc.
- ☐ The office doesn't have enough open space, limiting communication; or it has too much, creating a lack of privacy.
- ☐ The furniture is too large or small and is not efficiently laid out.
- ☐ You have too much storage space or not enough.
- ☐ The server/telecom/data room is too small or too large.
- ☐ You have other functionally obsolete spaces (training rooms, libraries, mail/copy rooms, etc.).

### 7. The building is wrong.

- ☐ It's not professional enough—the employees of other companies in the building wear jeans and T-shirts,

4

while your staff comes to work in suits or business casual attire.

☐ It doesn't give the right kind of "wow" factor to clients, employees or potential new hires.

☐ There are too many columns.

☐ The windows are too small.

☐ The floor plate layout is not conducive to how your business groups interact with one another.

☐ The building lacks amenities (parking, fitness center, cafeteria, conference center, bike storage, restaurants, roof deck, etc.).

## 8. The building location is wrong.

☐ Your business community has shifted to a new sub-market.

☐ Your labor force lives too far from the current location.

☐ Public transportation or highways have shifted and changed how easy it is for employees to commute to the office.

☐ Parking is scarce or too expensive within the near vicinity.

## 9. There is no road map for future growth or contraction in your current building.

☐ It's too small and just doesn't have more available space.

☐ The larger tenants in the building have long-term leases on adjacent space.

☐ Staying in your current building works for the short term, but not for the future.

☐ The floor plate size or configuration makes it difficult to expand or contract.

## 10. General hassles.

- ☐ Poor HVAC.
- ☐ Poor IT cabling or Internet connectivity.
- ☐ Poor lighting.
- ☐ Poor electricity.
- ☐ Poor security.
- ☐ Poor janitorial.
- ☐ Building management or ownership is not responsive or effective.
- ☐ Inefficient power.
- ☐ Unpleasant smells or sounds (I've seen it all, including pigeons, leaks, mold, you name it).

The list could go on and on, but I hope you're able to identify several key data points to help you pinpoint your own Deficiency Drivers. Don't be alarmed if you checked most every box— clearly you need to move! At the same time, don't be surprised if you only checked a few. Hopefully that means you'll have added clarity in the next chapter when we think through your Success Factors. Before we move on, please write down any other Deficiency Drivers you may be experiencing that are not listed above.

1. _____

   _____

2. _____

   _____

3. _____

   _____

4. _____

   _____

5. _____

   _____

As we wrap up this chapter on what's not ideal and your Deficiency Drivers, here is a summary of what to keep top of mind so you develop a thorough strategy and avoid costly mistakes.

- ☑ Think critically about the work being done in your office, how your teams interact and how your office space impacts or impedes your potential. You'll be surprised by how many processes are designed around the physical attributes of your space as opposed to the physical attributes of your space being designed to support your ideal processes.

- ☑ Engage employees from different departments and seniorities to glean their perspectives. Simple surveys can be an effective tool to draw out Deficiency Drivers.

- ☑ Study the transportation and commuting patterns of your workforce—you may be surprised by what you learn. Your real estate advisor should have sophisticated software to help you analyze this if you send him or her the zip codes of your employees.

- ☑ Call people in your network or in your industry to learn about what strategies they have implemented to solve their real estate challenges.

# STEP 2

# *What Are Your Success Factors?*

*Envisioning what needs to happen during the course of your office leasing process to make it a huge success.*

Just thinking through the previous chapter on what's not ideal and identifying your Deficiency Drivers should help you clarify what would indeed be ideal. In fact, if you've thought through your specific situation, you're likely 80 percent of the way to determining what's best for your physical office space and your financial, qualitative or cultural drivers.

And with those pain points out of the way, you now have room to cast vision—to really connect the direction of your business with the needs of an office space. I will borrow a technique from Dan Sullivan, creator of The Strategic Coach® Program, to explore this next concept:

Imagine you and I are sitting in your brand new office space in the future (or your same office space with a newly re-negotiated lease) and we are looking back on today. The project is complete, leases are signed, construction is finished, everyone has moved in and your organization is poised for huge success. What has to have happened during the project for you and your leadership team to really feel thrilled about the progress you've made?

In other words: *What are your Success Factors?*

Identifying your Success Factors frames the high-level goals of your project: What is most important to you, to your team, to your board or to your investors? Think beyond the small details and dream big. If you could redefine your culture—the way your employees interact, work and feel engaged—what changes would you make?

The best way to give your Success Factors a little clarity is through some real-life examples that my clients have shared with me:

- We want to reduce our annual occupancy costs by 20 percent.
- We want to increase our seat count by 250 people with the opportunity to grow by an additional 250 people in five years.
- We want to move from a model where everyone has a dedicated seat to a completely "free-addressing" model where desks are shared and no one has a dedicated office or work station.
- We want to renew our lease for 10 years and lock in below-market rents, without having to pay any out-of-pocket capital expenditure (capex) costs for construction, furniture or technology.
- We want to get rid of our terrible furniture from the 1980s and finally have a boardroom where we can proudly invite clients (Maybe they should have put that '80s furniture in storage; I'm sure it won't be long before it's back in again!).
- We want to move to a different part of the city that has quick access to the highway and retail for our employ-

ees to run out and grab lunch.

- We want to transition our partners from three-size offices to a universal-size (i.e. one-size) office, which will reduce our space by 15 percent and allow us to reinvest the savings into our servers, phones and mobile technology.
- We want to reduce physical file storage by 50 percent and go as paperless as possible.

I'd encourage you to take a moment to brainstorm what Success Factors come to mind for your upcoming project in the space provided below.

1. _____

_____

2. _____

_____

3. _____

_____

4. _____

_____

5. _____

_____

Once you and the other decision makers in your organization think through your Success Factors, you must prioritize them and—just as importantly—assign a priority weight to them in a simple Excel chart. These Success Factors will become your North Star when determining which building and space you'll select.

Below is an example Success Factor Weighted Matrix for reference. I'm including values for three different buildings so you can see how this matrix would look at the end of the process. Note: 3 is the best, and 1 is less ideal. We take the values for each Success Factor (i.e. 1, 2 or 3), multiply them by the Priority Weight and then add them up for a total score.

| Success Factor | Priority Weight | Building A | Building B | Building C |
|---|---|---|---|---|
| Low rent | 40% | 3 | 2 | 3 |
| Lease term less than 3 years | 30% | 2 | 2 | 1 |
| Furniture included | 15% | 1 | 3 | 1 |
| Room for expansion | 15% | 1 | 3 | 2 |
| Total | 100% | 2.1 | 2.3 | 1.95 |

Here's a great example of how Success Factors evolve as a company grows:

In 2010, five senior-level consultants decided to break away from their company and start their own firm. They were referred to me, and they asked for my help in advising them with their first, small office. During their first two projects in 2010 and 2011, their Success Factors were clear:

1.  Short-term lease.
2.  Low rent.
3.  Little to no capex, with furniture included.
4.  Room for expansion.
5.  Professional feel but not extravagant.
6.  Centrally located to public transportation to attract new college grads who did not drive to work.

Together, we found subleases in both instances that checked all of those boxes. They were only in their first subleased space for 12 months prior to moving into a second, larger sublease the next year. With subleases, however, you have to live with what someone else has designed, which can leave you feeling the space is not totally your own. So in 2014, having grown to 65 employees with plans to increase to 100, my clients were leaning toward a custom design of their own space. This time around their Success Factors were quite different. Now they wanted to:

1.  Build out new space while limiting any construction and furniture-related costs as much as possible.
2.  Increase their building image without significant rental increases.
3.  Design a space that fit their working style with high

levels of mobility that included free-addressing and so-phisticated technology in conference rooms for team collaboration.
4. Maintain flexibility to contract, expand or terminate their lease if their business drastically changed or they decided to sell it.

After a nine-month process, the project came down to re-newing and expanding in their older space or relocating to new space in one of two buildings. Here is how their final Success Factor Weighted Matrix looked:

| Success Factor | Priority Weight | Renew & Expand | Relocate 3 Blocks Away | Relocate Across Street |
|---|---|---|---|---|
| Limit Capex | 30% | 3 | 3 | 3 |
| Good Building Image With Moderate Annual Rent | 30% | 2 | 2 | 3 |
| High Level of Mobility | 20% | 1 | 3 | 3 |
| Future Flexibility | 20% | 1 | 3 | 3 |
| **Total** | **100%** | **1.9** | **2.7** | **3** |

The choice was clear, and all five partners agreed that re-locating to the building right across the street was the right solution. Here's what they got:

- A 10-year lease for 100 people with an option to expand into an adjacent space three years later to accommodate 30 additional seats, and terminate the lease at the end of the seventh year.
- Even within the initial floor plan, the opportunity to add 15 more seats through a slight modification to the furniture layout.
- The owner of their new building constructed the space to my clients' design specifications and even included furniture.
- We secured a below-market rent right before the building was sold to a new owner who later increased rental rates dramatically for future tenants.
- The building was rated Class A-, and it had a newly renovated lobby, fitness and conference center, but it wasn't so extravagant that their clients would question whether their hourly consulting rates were too high.
- The building was within three blocks of every major commuter train station in the city, with covered parking right across the street.

In this particular project all four Success Factors fell beautifully into place (which is not always the case—many projects have to compromise on at least one or two).

I visited their new offices in late 2014, and as they walked me around with glowing pride, we took a few minutes to stop and talk in their new café. It was stunning! There were dramatic floor-to-ceiling windows, 12-foot-high exposed ceilings, a big kitchen with bar stools and a keg in the back (for consumption only after business hours, of course). They chose to give the café, and therefore their employees, the best view in the entire office overlooking a beautiful plaza in downtown Chicago. What a cultural statement!

"Does this café get used?" I asked. "Absolutely!" they said. "We have an agreement in our culture that no one can eat lunch at their desk. If someone has a call during lunchtime, they sit in one of the small phone booth/team rooms next to the café. This was a total game changer for us. Our young consultants sit and eat with the highest-level managing directors in the office. Relationships are built, and people feel appreciated because they get to enjoy the light and air from the best part of the entire floor." They went on to tell me about all the parties, cocktail hours, client events and all-company meetings they held in the café.

And then they said something that really stuck with me: "Shared experiences. It's all about creating a place for our employees to have shared *experiences* with their coworkers and our clients. That creates the fabric of our culture and the strength of our community."

These clients understood their Success Factors, and they knew when it was time to invest in their culture. It was the right moment in their growth trajectory where they could make a commitment longer than two to three years, and the results paid off with dividends. Let them be a model for you.

As we wrap up this chapter on Success Factors, here is a summary of what to keep top of mind so you develop a thorough strategy and avoid costly mistakes.

☑ Build consensus with key stakeholders on your Success Factors at the beginning of the project to avoid prioritizing less important details of a future office space over the core needs of your business.

☑ Get everyone's goals out on the table early, and document the Success Factor Weighted Matrix as a reference point to look back on in the future.

☑ Have an ideal lease term in mind based on the stability of your business and your willingness to invest capital in your space.

☑ Technology is drastically changing the way we work, with more employees working from home, requiring less personal space for paper files, sharing "free-addressing" desks and functioning with high levels of mobility. The real estate industry is calling this concept "Workplace Strategy." Think critically about your business and your industry and how this could impact your traditional ways of working in your office. I can't emphasize enough the impact changes in technology will continue to have on workplace design.

☑ Explain your goals and challenges to your outside team of advisors (we'll cover team formation in Step Four) and encourage them to find creative real estate solutions that match your business. The goal is to design a strategy around your business, not around what is "typical" in the market.

# KICKING OFF YOUR OFFICE LEASE

# STEP 3

# *What Are Your Scenarios?*

*Identifying the most likely real estate scenarios that match the needs of your organization.*

Once my clients have thought through their Deficiency Drivers and have identified, prioritized and assigned weights to their most important Success Factors, they have a very good sense of how their office leasing project might unfold. Potential real estate solutions naturally begin falling into place, which brings us to Kick-Off Question Three: What Are Your Scenarios?

I have outlined the most typical examples of real estate scenarios below. Your scenario will come with many of its own nuances, but for the sake of simplicity I've included the most common cases you'll encounter. Please check those that apply to your situation.

- ☐ Open a new office (if this is the first office in a particular city).
- ☐ Renegotiate and renew your existing lease.
- ☐ Renegotiate and renew your existing lease and downsize.

- ☐ Renegotiate and renew your existing lease and expand.
- ☐ Expand within the same building or another building and maintain your existing lease.
- ☐ Terminate all or a portion of your existing lease.
- ☐ Relocate within the same building or building complex on another floor.
- ☐ Relocate to another building.
- ☐ Sublease a portion of your existing space and stay in what remains.
- ☐ Sublease your entire space and relocate to another building.
- ☐ Purchase a building or develop a building from the ground up.

Are there any scenarios that are not on the list above that you'd consider? If so, feel free to jot them down:

1. _____

_____

2. _____

_____

3. _____

_____

4. _____

_____

5. _____

_____

Here's an example of how one of my clients in the insurance industry analyzed their occupancy scenarios and arrived at the best solution for their needs. It gets a little complicated, so get ready to focus!

Back in 2002, an insurance company signed a 10-year lease for 50,000 square feet. When I met them in 2010, their lease was two and a half years from expiring, and how they were using their space was drastically different from how it was originally designed in 2002. Over that time period, they relocated many of their administrative functions to other cities, their need for an onsite data center shrank by 75 percent, their office size standards dropped by 20 percent, and their space was tired in so many ways. After consulting with an architect, they determined that they only needed about 40,000 square feet. So we focused on four scenarios:

1. Renegotiate and renew their lease for 50,000 square feet.
2. Relocate to 40,000 square feet in another building.
3. Relocate to 40,000 square feet on another floor in the same building.
4. Renegotiate their lease and downsize to 40,000 square feet on the same floor.

Before we jump into how they worked through each of their scenarios, let's touch on their key Deficiency Drivers and Success Factors:

# DEFICIENCY DRIVERS:

- Too much space.
- High rental rate due to 10 years of annual rent escala-

tions, coupled with a downturn in the economy which drove market rents down.

- Location on the periphery of the central business district with longer commute times for certain train riders.
- Older finishes and design elements.
- Too much open work station space and not enough executive office space, due to moving many administrative functions to another city.
- Too large of a server room.
- Inadequate conference rooms for all-company meetings and client training functions, including a need for more up-to-date audio/visual capabilities (video conferencing, microphones and speakers in the ceiling).
- Inefficient office and conference room design with curved walls and meandering hallways.
- Lack of natural light to their open areas and limited glass on exterior offices or conference rooms.

## SUCCESS FACTORS (Weighted by priority):

1. Reduce the size of the space and increase efficiency of the design and build-out (35 percent).
2. Reduce the per-square-foot (PSF) rental rate by 20 percent per year (25 percent).
3. Limit capex (20 percent):
   a. In a renegotiation/renewal scenario, the goal was zero capex over and above the tenant improvement allowance received from the owner so that any free rent could be applied directly to cash.
   b. In a relocation, the goal was to design professional, yet affordable space so that any free rent would

fully offset the capex spend over and above the tenant improvement allowance received from the owner.

4. Negotiate further rights to contract, terminate or expand portions of the space in the future (20 percent).

With that said, let's see how they analyzed their four scenarios.

## SCENARIO #1:
### Renegotiate and renew their lease for 50,000 square feet.

At first glance, renewing their old 50,000 square foot lease may have been the simplest and most sensible option. If they opted to downsize to 40,000 square feet instead, the accompanying costs would really add up once they started construction and reconfigured electric, lighting, HVAC, etc.

They had to weigh the difference between (a) the high capex and hassle involved with living through construction to downsize by 20 percent to 40,000 square feet and (b) paying for 20 percent extra square footage they didn't really need, but not spending the capex. This type of a/b analysis seems simple, but it was one of the most complicated choices they faced because of the number of decisions and budgets required to understand where they would land along the capex and square footage spectrum.

After studying this scenario, they concluded that they couldn't justify paying for 20 percent too much space that wasn't laid out to suit the needs of their business. We struck Scenario #1 from the list.

## SCENARIO #2:
### Relocate to 40,000 square feet in another building.

They began to think they might be better off financially and culturally by relocating to a more affordable space for 40,000 square feet in another building and constructing a new space from scratch. We found three comparable buildings with superior access to commuter trains and amenities, equally efficient floor plates with good natural light and few columns. The three buildings offered competitive deal terms including low rental rates and high concession packages that included free rent and tenant improvement allowances. Scenario #2 was a solid contender.

## SCENARIO #3:
### Relocate to 40,000 square feet on another floor in the same building.

They prepared test-fit plans (high-level architectural plans) and budgets to relocate to a lower floor in their current building, but the light and views there were far inferior to what they'd enjoyed the last 10 years on their higher floors. A lack of daylight was not a concession they were willing to make—even considering the cheaper rental rates in the lower floors. The lower floors would also require a build-out from scratch, so from a capex perspective they would be better off spending that money on another building that had better light and views. We scratched Scenario #3 from the list.

# SCENARIO #4:
## Renegotiate their lease and downsize to 40,000 square feet.

As I mentioned before, it was very expensive to redesign and shrink the footprint of the original space by 10,000 square feet, but after further consideration, they concluded that they would go to their board of directors and propose that the savings from leasing 40,000 vs. 50,000 square feet over the life of a new 10-year lease would offset the added capex to complete the project. Their biggest challenge was that the building's owner did not want to provide a large tenant improvement allowance for existing tenants. The owner had only budgeted large allowances to attract new tenants to the building.

After nine months of negotiations and convincing the owner my client was about to relocate to another building (this was not a bluff; we had a letter of intent ready to be signed down the street), the owner offered a tenant improvement allowance that could sufficiently pay for the construction required to downsize to 40,000 square feet. Scenario #4 was the winner! My client felt the same joy that many of us feel when we watch the Dunkin' Donuts' donut vs. bagel vs. coffee race. Just like those Dunkin' Donuts races, complex real estate decisions are often very uncertain until the very end of the process.

Here is how their Success Factor Weighted Matrix looked for the project:

| Success Factor | Weight | Renew Lease 50,000 SF | Relocate to New Building 40,000 SF | Relocate in Same Building 40,000 SF | Renew Lease 40,000 SF |
|---|---|---|---|---|---|
| Reduce Size, Increase Efficiency | 35% | 1 | 3 | 3 | 3 |
| Reduce PSF Cost | 25% | 3 | 3 | 3 | 3 |
| Limit Capex | 20% | 2 | 1 | 1 | 2 |
| Future Flexibility | 20% | 2 | 3 | 3 | 3 |
| Total | 100% | 1.9 | 2.6 | 2.6 | 2.8 |

Note: 3 is the best, 1 is less ideal

I go into a lot of detail in this example to stress the fact that many sophisticated factors go into analyzing these types of larger projects. This particular client was committing to a multi-million dollar lease obligation over a 10-year period and a construction budget of several million dollars.

From a non-financial perspective, this project was success-ful in that it gave them a cultural "fresh start." Since they'd relocated some of their administrative functions to another city during the financial recession of 2008-2010, the office felt somewhat empty. A new design, coupled with a commitment to a new 10-year lease, sent a powerful message to their employees that the company was committed to maintaining a strong presence in this location and to rebuilding a new culture for the future.

You will note each of the four scenarios have very different strategies, timelines and budgets, but whether you are dealing with an office for 25 employees or 5,000, one critical need remains the same: assembling a seasoned team to evaluate each of the scenarios, run a thorough vetting process and execute the final plan. In the next chapter, we'll cover team formation.

As we wrap up this chapter on your Scenarios, here is a summary of what to keep top of mind so you develop a thorough strategy and avoid costly mistakes.

☑ Deal terms such as rental rates, rent escalations, free rent and tenant improvement allowances can be estimated and substantiated by market comps, even at the beginning of a project. Construction costs are often the most challenging pieces in the puzzle to determine. You'll be well served to patiently put together good budgets prior to making any final decisions.

☑ Your Scenarios will be largely impacted by what stage you find yourself in the market cycle. Are rents increasing or decreasing, what is the available supply for space in your size range, what is a particular owner's goals, etc.? Understanding market dynamics and each owner's goals will help you focus your energy—and save you time—by analyzing scenarios that align with your needs and the market realities.

☑ Once you pick your final scenario, you'll agree to a "Letter of Intent," also known as a "Term Sheet," and then the attorneys will begin drafting legal, binding documents. Until you agree to a Letter of Intent, and sometimes even during lease negotiations, it is prudent to have a backup option that is fully vetted just in case your No. 1 option falls through.

# STEP 4

# *Who Is On Your Team?*

*Selecting the internal and external players you need to orchestrate a successful office leasing process.*

L ike anything in life, you can have a clear mission and vision, but if you don't have the right team in place to make it happen, you'll be in big trouble. Throughout your office leasing process, many team members may touch the project: the C-Suite, leadership team, board, HR, IT, finance, office manager, real estate advisor, architect, project manager, general contractor, engineers, move vendors, audio/visual vendors, furniture vendors, telecom/data vendors, phone vendors and others.

To keep things simple here, we're only going to focus on the core internal and external team members you need to help kick off your office leasing strategy.

## INTERNAL TEAM MEMBERS

Every organization is different. But what is consistent across most successful leasing projects is that the internal leaders need to have credibility within their organizations, access to decision makers, consensus building skills, adequate time and enough attention to detail.

Some of my clients only have one primary internal team leader, and some have three. I'd say most projects have two co-leaders. There's no magic number, but my experience has taught me that one person doesn't have the time and full skill set to do everything on the project, and with three co-leaders there might be too many cooks in the kitchen.

Using two co-leaders as an example, they usually divide their roles between a Strategy-Oriented Leader and an Action-Oriented Leader. Neither role is more or less important, but they are quite different.

## Strategy-Oriented Leader

Think of who will be standing up in the final approval meeting presenting the options to your leadership team, board, partnership or the equivalent decision-making body. This person understands the strategic initiatives of your organization and typically has the higher seniority of the project co-leaders. The Strategy-Oriented Leader is often involved in the following:

- Strategy development.
- Team formation.
- Building tours.
- Negotiations.
- Budget review.
- Building selection.
- Legal review.
- Design direction.

## Action-Oriented Leader

Think of someone who typically takes on implementing complex, strategic initiatives within your company. This is a person who has the ability, time and relationships within the organization to roll up his or her sleeves and dig into the details of the project. This person is involved in all phases outlined above and will be very closely involved with:

- Handling all contracts.
- Managing all emails.
- Directing the details of the project and meeting with all internal departments and outside vendors.
- Bringing specific decisions (large and small) to broader leadership for their signoff/approval.
- Preparing for key meetings with broader leadership.
- Handling the finer details of design, construction, moving and coordinating with accounting, finance, HR and IT.
- Managing communication with broader employees.
- Ensuring the Strategy-Oriented Leader gets what they need (deliverables, data, etc.) in advance of each meeting.

## Other Internal Team Members

To support your Strategy-Oriented and Action-Oriented Leaders, you'll need a few more internal team members to weigh in on the early conversations and throughout the process:

### Finance/Accounting.

Make sure your CFO or relevant finance/accounting resources are able to cover:
- Budget planning and forecasting.

- Understanding any tax implications for capex and depreciation (construction, furniture, etc.).
- Understanding how accounting for the project will be handled (cash or accrual/GAAP—if you don't know what this means, just ask your finance person if the lease costs will be accounted for on a cash or accrual/GAAP basis).
- Any existing un-depreciated assets or write-offs that will impact the financial statements.
- Discussion around leasing versus owning, which could lead to complicated analyses related to financing and optimal deal structures. Although this book focuses on leases, larger projects should consider alternate deal structures which your real estate advisor can discuss with you.

**IT.** Consult your tech team on:

- IT and audiovisual budgets, specifically what will be upgraded and what will need to be moved.
- Server room requirements (size, wiring/cabling, back-up power, security, need for supplemental cooling if necessary).
- Location of higher-power machines, such as copy machines, which will require different electrical outlets.
- Timing to set up new voice and Internet service from the telecom provider (in the case of a relocation).

**HR.** Make sure your human resources team has a handle on:

- Headcount projections.
- Specific business groups that will grow or shrink quicker than other business groups.

- Location considerations related to commuting patterns of both existing and potential new employees.
- Generational shifts of a changing workforce and its impact on the space design, technology and hiring goals.

**Legal**. Your legal team will be valuable to confirm:

- Questions related to specific clauses in the lease.
- Restoration obligations, including furniture or other elements of the space that need to be removed or restored to the original turnover condition when your lease expires.
- Notification requirements for communicating critical dates or information to the landlord.

As I mentioned before, many team members will have a hand in your office leasing project, but the inside team members listed above are your core. So now let's move on to your external team.

## EXTERNAL TEAM MEMBERS

### Real Estate Advisor

The first External Team Member you'll want to bring on board is the commercial real estate broker/advisor. The real estate advisor's job is to quarterback the entire process. They should be involved from the very early stages of developing the external team through the building selection, negotiations, lease execution, design and construction, move-in and construction punch-list items. Think of the real estate advisor as your outsourced real estate department.

Here's my recommended process for engaging a real estate advisor:

### Hold introductory meetings.

Meet with three to four real estate advisory firms for 45 minutes to one hour each. You'll benefit from meeting with large, medium and boutique firms.

The purpose of these meetings is not so much for you to select a real estate advisor (although you might), but to ask questions, explain your situation and get their feedback, and get answers to specific questions you have about the market and real estate process. If you're in a time crunch and your company doesn't require a long procurement process, you can make this introductory meeting the final interview. If that's the case, follow some of the recommendations I outline in this chapter in the formal face-to-face interview section for each meeting.

### Get requests for proposals (if necessary).

If you have a more formal procurement process, you may be required to send out a request for proposal (RFP) or a request for information (RFI) prior to having final face-to-face interviews. If you have to go down this path and you would like to see sample RFP/RFI questions for real estate services, feel free to email me at **jon@kickingoffyourofficelease.com**, and I can send you an example list of specific questions.

### Conduct formal face-to-face interviews.

If your process is a bit more formal such that you can't hire a real estate advisor based on an initial meeting—but perhaps it isn't so formal that you have to issue a formal RFP/RFI—you'll probably choose to have formal interviews with the final candidate firms prior to making a final decision. I encourage you to narrow your final list of candidates down to two or three. To make the most of your face-to-face interviews, I recommend the following:

- Prepare a list of questions you want each real estate firm to discuss during the meeting and send the list to each firm prior to the meeting.
- Send candidates your lease, your lease invoice and a description of your primary Deficiency Drivers and four to five Success Factors. You should sign a confidentiality agreement prior to sending the lease information.
- During the meeting, ask for creative ideas and solutions to your challenges—not just an overview of the real estate firm and their experience.
- Make sure all your important decision makers are in the room during interviews. If your CEO or other critical leaders will not be actively involved in the ongoing project, they still may want to be involved during the real estate advisor selection and then at the end of the leasing process to tour the final shortlist of buildings.
- Plan on taking a morning or an afternoon to interview all of the firms for one hour each.

Each market across the country and the world is different, but in general, the criteria for selecting a real estate advisor is consistent. Some areas you may want to inquire about during the interview include:

- Experience in your local market.
- Experience with your building's owner.
- Experience with similar projects.
- Experience within your industry.

- Ensuring that the real estate advisory team at the table will be the actual team running the project. You don't want to be sold by one person and then handed off to another.
- What value they place on trust, integrity and relationships for the long term. This is a tough one to flush out, but it shouldn't be overlooked.
- Credibility and experience in the market. Ask for references and call them, call other people you may know in their industry or network or look at their client lists and call people you know at those companies. You may also want to talk to people at other companies who did not engage a particular real estate advisor to understand why.
- Other resources offered or included in their services. Services might include project (construction) management services, incentive negotiations expertise, workplace strategy consulting (engaged prior to an architect on a complex project to study your working environment), mapping and demographics, labor analytics, financial analysis consulting, portfolio analytics software, data center or colocation services, or move management.

Once you've selected a firm, ask them to send an engagement agreement that should be negotiated prior to kicking off the project. In the U.S., when a lease is signed, brokers are paid by the landlord as either a percentage of the lease value or with a fixed rate multiplied by the square footage and the years of lease term. In international markets, the broker can be paid by the tenant and it varies from country to country. If your project involves a sublease, the sublandlord pays the subleasing fee. Whatever the case, make sure you thoroughly understand the compensation process in your market.

## Architect

Hiring an architect early on in the process depends on your Success Factors and the size of your project. Very rarely do real estate service firms have in-house architects, so you should assume that you'll have to go to a third party.

The rule of thumb in my experience is that projects that are 10,000 square feet or smaller usually rely on the building's own architect to manage the design process. The challenge there is that the architect is working for the landlord, so you have to be very careful about "dotting every i and crossing every t" to ensure that your interests are well represented. With these "turnkey projects," the tenant works directly with the building owner and the owner's architect to define a construction scope. If the landlord manages the construction, architects are usually paid by the landlord, and the tenant will pay for construction costs that are over and above the mutually agreed upon scope and budget.

Projects larger than 10,000 square feet or that are particularly complicated in scope usually require that you hire your own architect who works directly for you throughout the entire process. The architectural process begins with the strategy development "Programming" phase, where the architect studies the way you work and estimates the size and layout of your ideal future space. This often involves questionnaires and one-on-one interviews with your key stakeholders to understand how the business functions, what departments need to be adjacent to one another, what the growth projections are and what the technology needs will be.

The architect will then work with the real estate advisor and the broader external team to study each potential building and space. The landlords will offer you a construction allowance ("Tenant Improvement Allowance" or "TI Allowance") that you can spend at your discretion, with some potential caveats as to how much of the allowance must be spent on actual construction. If the tenant manages the construction, architects are almost always paid by the tenant with funds that come out of the TI Allowance.

After you engage a real estate advisor, ask him or her whether you should focus on a landlord turnkey project where you use the building architect or if you should hire an architect at the start of the project. Every market and building is different, but most importantly you want to create the right strategy for your specific situation.

Let's assume for discussion purposes that you will hire your own architect. If you don't already have several in your network to choose from, your real estate advisor can manage the interview process for you and give recommendations. We usually interview three architects. If you have a more formal process, you can send out an RFP or RFI prior to scheduling three live presentations. If your real estate advisor doesn't have an architectural RFP template, please reach out to me at **jon@kickingoffyourofficelease.com** and I'll send you some examples. If your process is less formal and doesn't require an RFP process, you can just schedule a three-hour block of time with three 45 minute to an hour interviews.

Here are some areas to focus on when selecting an architect:

- Experience with commercial office interior projects is a must. You wouldn't commission your home plumber to design and install the kitchen in your 200,000 square foot office. If you know someone in the architecture industry, but neither they nor their firm focuses on commercial office interiors, I do not recommend hiring them.

- Experience in your particular industry is a plus.
- Experience with other firms of your size or complexity is another plus.
- Get the right price for your project. Unlike brokers, for whom fees are generally the same and dictated by landlords, architecture fees vary greatly. Your real estate advisor can work with you to negotiate fees prior to signing a formal engagement agreement.
- Team formation for architects is largely based on their workload, so clearly identify your project schedule and confirm the architecture firms can provide a team with availability when you need it.

The most important part about selecting an architect, and other External Team Members, is confirming that you will get senior level leadership during the entire process. You do not want the project to be handed down to a less experienced professional. Make this very clear during your interviews and in your engagement agreements.

## Project Manager

Some of my clients have in-house personnel with construction management experience, but most do not. Depending on the size and scope of your project, you may consider hiring a project manager whose job is to manage the budget and schedule. The priority of the project manager is clear and simple: to complete the project on (or under) budget and on (or ahead of) schedule.

All project vendors will report to the project manager. Vendors typically include architects, general contractors, audio/visual (AV) consultants, mechanical electrical and plumbing

(MEP) engineers, move vendors, furniture vendors, telecom/ data vendors, phone vendors, security consultants, signage vendors and others.

The project manager will work with you to select each vendor and consultant and act as your outsourced construction management arm throughout the process. They will review all contracts with the vendors, manage weekly meetings, provide meeting minutes, review all budgets throughout the project and lead the entire design and construction team. If you do hire a project manager, hire them before you hire an architect so they can help you throughout the architectural interview and on-boarding process.

Often your real estate advisor will have a project management arm within their company and can tack on this expertise as a part of their service offering. If your real estate advisor does not have project management expertise within their company, or if their project managers are not best-in-class, you should interview third-party project managers as well.

My rule of thumb is that I encourage my clients to engage a project manager for projects larger than 10,000 rentable square feet that will require moderate to heavy construction. Project managers are paid by the tenant with funds that come out of the TI Allowance. Their fees might range from 1 percent to 3 percent of the total project budget, but their value typically pays for their services three-to-fourfold (or more).

As for areas to focus on during project management interviews, you can largely use the same list I outlined in the architecture interview section. Place special emphasis on the project manager's relationships within the design and construction community and how their relationships will help you to leverage the best pricing and vendor commitment throughout your project.

My final advice on External Team formation for your office leasing process may be the most important of all:

**Do not compromise on credibility, integrity, values or honesty.**

Your External Team represents you to the market. They will be speaking on your behalf, reflecting your brand and advocating for your interests. Choose people who align with your culture and your values. They will be a part of your team, so be patient in your selection, do your research, vet out references and choose your teammates wisely.

As we wrap up this chapter on your Internal and External Teams, here is a summary of what to keep top of mind so you develop a thorough strategy and avoid costly mistakes.

☑ Some organizations are very democratic, and others seek the input of a smaller group of decision makers. Either route is fine, so long as the decision making process is discussed at the beginning of your project. When developing your Internal Team and the associated internal influencers, make sure that there is a clear leader. The buck needs to stop with someone. Too many cooks in the kitchen can lead to a very slow, painful, inefficient process.

☑ When developing your External Team, think through the broader needs of your portfolio. Do you have or will you have multiple office locations? Do you have real estate needs that are not office related (industrial, retail, data center, facilities management,etc.)? Would you benefit from working with a partner who has resources in each of those markets or areas of expertise?

☑ Even if you have worked with a real estate advisor, architect or project manager in the past, it is good to re-interview on a periodic basis. Markets, personnel and resources are constantly changing, and you don't want a prior relationship to cost you money.

# STEP 5

# *What Is Your Schedule?*

*Plotting your timeline to reach a successful outcome.*

Now we'll explore three different stages of the leasing process and how long each one takes. They are:

1. **Strategy Development:** Your schedule related to defining the project goals and developing an external team.
2. **Market Engagement:** Your schedule related to identifying and analyzing market options and budgets, negotiating deal terms and signing a lease.
3. **Design, Construction and Move-in:** Your schedule related to the design, permit, construction and move-in after signing a lease.

All three of these areas are affected by the complexity and size of your project. In order to keep every available scenario on the table during a real estate process, we design our schedules based on the scenario with the longest timeline, which is usually the relocation to space that requires a full construction project from scratch. Based on market dynamics, this can even include buildings that are under construction or still in the development stage.

On the next page is a chart which provides rule-of-thumb schedule estimates broken out by project size. I am using an average rentable square foot per seat ratio of 200 for discussion purposes. For example: A company with 50 employees would require approximately 10,000 rentable square feet. Different industries will use more or less space based on their needs—open-plan tech companies gravitate closer to 150 rentable square feet per seat, while other users that require more dedicated offices or conferencing spaces may lean toward 250 to 300 square feet per seat—but this formula of 200 square feet per seat is a nice, simple base to start from.

Please include a buffer at the beginning of the project based on the estimated time required to interview and formally engage a real estate advisor, which should happen prior to Strategy Development. Once the clock starts ticking on Strategy Development, the assumption is that your internal team is solidified and your real estate advisor is on board. The other external team members are hired during the Strategy Development phase (architect, project management, other workplace strategy consultants, incentives consultants, labor analysis consultants, etc.).

**STEP 5:** *What Is Your Schedule?*

| # of Employees | Est. SF | Develop Strategy | Engage Market | Design, Construction & Move-in | Total |
|---|---|---|---|---|---|
| 5-20 | 1,000 - 4,000 | 0.5 | 2 | 3.5 | 6 |
| 20-50 | 4,000 - 10,000 | 2 | 4 | 6 | 12 |
| 50-100 | 10,000 - 20,000 | 2 | 6 | 8 | 16 |
| 100-250 | 20,000 - 50,000 | 3 | 8 | 9 | 20 |
| 250-1,000 | 50,000 - 200,000 | 4 | 10 | 12 | 26 |
| 1,000 + | 200,000 + | 4 | 10 | 18 | 32 |

Note: The schedule is based on months.

There is no cookie-cutter way to develop a comprehensive schedule for most projects of size, but I hope the table above gives you some high-level parameters to think through how much time you should allocate. If a project requires little to no construction and the "perfect" space is identified on the first tour, the entire process might only take two months. Here are some practical reasons why it takes longer to execute a larger project:

- Obtaining city permits and completing design and construction often takes longer than anticipated.
- Large tenants are making decisions several years in ad-

vance of their lease expirations. If an owner of a building is aware that one of their large tenants is relocating in the future, they will begin marketing their space immediately. To be proactive, a wise tenant should start the process early and be aware of what spaces are opening up in the future.

- Smaller tenants of less than 10,000 square feet often sign shorter-term leases in the three-to-seven year range, so owners are used to constant turnover and less downtime between one tenant's lease expiration and the next tenant's lease commencement. Larger tenants often sign longer term leases in the 10-to-15 year range. Some owners would rather wait to find the right tenant who can make a long-term commitment, even if it means committing to a lease commencement well into the future and going many months without rent prior to the new tenant's lease commencing.

- Larger tenants are more likely to sign leases in buildings that are under development or under construction, which requires an earlier commitment.

Once you engage your real estate advisor, he or she will work with you to develop a very detailed schedule with key milestones for each phase of the project.

## DEFINING THE NEED

Sometimes the most challenging part of your schedule is convincing your leadership team that there is actually a need to change your leasing situation!

The schedules provided above commence once an organization has acknowledged there is a need that should be further explored. Keep that in mind as you are managing internal expectations within your organization. For some of our more nimble clients, consensus around a need can be achieved in five minutes. But for our clients with multiple stakeholders (law firms and other partnerships, international companies with multiple decision making levels, larger organizations, public institutions, private equity firms or joint ventures) it can take six to 12 months just to get approval to kick off the process.

Depending on the goals of your project, the actual drivers and needs could be very different. So the first question to ask yourself is: What is the need? Without a need, there's no reason to even consider a project. Some common needs are outlined below. They will likely match up with your Deficiency Drivers and Success Factors, which can be used to provide additional perspective:

**Lease expiration or opening a brand new office.**
Both of these needs are pretty easy to wrap your mind around. They're the most common type of projects.

**Need for more space even though there may be many years left on the lease.**
The biggest challenge for a growing company is for leadership to agree on the optimal flex point where the status quo just won't work anymore, balanced against the hesitancy to commit too early to a larger space that increases overhead too soon.

**A budget goal that must be achieved within a certain time frame that requires a sublease, lease termination or downsizing of space.**
For example, a business unit may find out on March 1 that they need to cut real estate costs by 25 percent prior to Dec. 31 of that same year. That gives them 10 months to develop and

execute on a strategy to renegotiate the lease, sublease space, etc. That schedule target is clear, so long as the directive from leadership is well defined and implemented.

**Mergers or acquisitions.**
M&A can be challenging due to the complexities associated with analyzing different business units, including personnel and IT synergies (or redundancies) within the two organizations. Confidentiality during the M&A due diligence process may also result in very delayed or hurried schedules in order to line up real estate options if and when the merger or acquisition closes. A real estate change is just one of the many organizational discussions after a merger or acquisition that requires a meeting of the minds, so make sure to add some extra time to the schedule in anticipation of a very slow decision making process.

**A termination option or a similar fixed option within the lease that must be analyzed.**
Lease rights such as termination, expansion or contraction options have critical impacts on schedules and need to be followed closely. Many options have notice periods of nine to 18 months. In these cases the notice date to exercise the option becomes the date that the Strategy Development and Market Engagement need to be completed in order to make a decision. Then the Design, Construction and Move-in processes can happen between the notice period and the effective date of the option.

Once you have a target date identified prior to which the need must be satisfied, you can build backwards from that date into the estimated starting date for the project.

## THE PROCESS

In the introduction of this book, I promised I wouldn't get too bogged down in the details of the process, but it is worth spending some time on what happens during each of the three stages. To make the process more practical, I will share a story of a client of mine whose need was driven by a termination right in their lease.

### Project Background

A professional services client of mine had a lease for 20,000 square feet expiring on July 31, 2018. They had a right to terminate the lease on Jan. 31, 2016 by providing written notice on Jan. 31, 2015. As we began strategizing around the project, we developed the following schedule:

Along with their notice of termination prior to Jan. 31, 2015, my client had to write a check to the landlord for $150,000, which, on a per-square-foot (PSF) basis, was only $7.50 PSF. My client was paying $30.00 PSF per year in rent, so the $7.50 PSF termination penalty equaled three months rent, which is a very low termination penalty.

From my client's and the landlord's perspective, the termination option date on Jan. 31, 2016 was essentially a lease expiration date should the tenant wish to pay the financial penalty, terminate the lease and move. Because the tenant had this fixed right to terminate, it created a clear date when the landlord likely would be willing to enter into a new negotiation. If my client didn't exercise the termination option prior to Jan. 31, 2015, the option simply would pass, and the lease naturally would expire on July 31, 2018.

If the lease were to be renegotiated, my client would not be required to pay the termination option penalty (i.e. not pay the $150,000), and they would extend the lease term past July 31, 2018, for a mutually agreed upon period of time. Since the termination option effective date was Jan. 31, 2016, the negotiation revolved around new lease terms (i.e. rental rate and other concessions) starting on Feb. 1, 2016. In exchange for my client waiving the termination option and extending the lease, they would expect some value in return from the landlord.

## Strategy Development: 4 Months

- The initial kick-off meeting included my client's co-founder, the COO, the general manager of the office and the head of IT. In that meeting we discussed some of their Deficiency Drivers, which we'd further discuss with the architect, and we brainstormed their key Success Factors. In addition, we provided them with an overview of the market, their owner, their most likely scenarios, the next steps for developing their external team, the proposed schedule and a high-level estimated budget for the project.
- Given the size of the project, we decided to hire our own architect as opposed to working with the landlord's architect. The client had an informal procurement process, and we engaged a local firm after two interviews with local architects.

- We supplemented the team by including a project manager from my company to manage the construction schedule and budget.
- During the second meeting with the client, we included the architect and the project manager.   This second meeting focused on further defining the Deficiency Drivers of the current space and discussing what the client's ideal space would look like should they move and start from scratch. A good portion of this meeting was spent discussing the future plans for the business and what changes would need to be made to the office space to support their future goals.
- After that meeting, the architect created a draft Program which summarized the client's needs in two scenarios: (1) renovating the existing space and (2) relocating to a new space. Both scenarios required approximately 15,000 to 17,000 usable square feet (also called USF, which is the usable space on the floor where employees can actually walk and work within the space), which equates to 18,000 to 20,000 rentable square feet (called RSF, which is the square footage on which the tenant pays rent that also includes the building lobby, corridors, bathrooms, etc.).
- This client needed to be located within close proximity to the airport, so although we studied their employee locations and commuting patterns, the location window they wanted to stay within was very small.

## Market Engagement: 10 Months

- Using 18,000 to 20,000 RSF as the target range, my team prepared a survey of all spaces in my client's preferred geographic range that could accommodate a lease commencement of Feb. 1, 2016, with occupancy on Sep. 1, 2015, for construction (150 days). We found only nine spaces since the client was very clear on what they wanted.

- After walking through the survey of nine options over the phone, we shortlisted the options down to six and toured them with the COO and the head of IT.
- After the tour, we further shortlisted the buildings and settled on the following scenarios:
  1. Renovate the existing space and renegotiate the lease.
  2. Relocate within the existing complex to another floor.
  3. Relocate to a new building (three different buildings were still in the mix).
- My team prepared a request for proposal (RFP) for each of the options, and we sent them to the client for their comments and approval prior to sending them to each of the respective landlords.
- Along with the RFP, we asked each landlord to pay our architect to prepare test fit plans. Each landlord agreed to pay up to $0.10 per RSF for the initial test fit and $0.05 per RSF for a revision. A test fit is a 2-D plan that shows how the client would lay out the space. It has nothing to do with the actual design elements, colors or finishes. It is just a black-and-white drawing that shows how the Program would fit in each space.
- The architect and our project manager toured the five options, and the architect worked on the test fits. Once the initial test fits were completed, we had a conference call with the client to review them and they provided high-level commentary on proposed revi-

sions. The architect revised the test fits, and then our project manager priced the plans with three different general contractors.

- Once I received the first-round proposals from the landlords, I worked with my financial analyst to create a financial model comparing the scenarios, which included the project manager's construction estimates. I also prepared a summary matrix of all of the non-financial proposal terms (expansion options, amenities, building security procedures, etc.) to simplify and streamline the client's review.

- The next meeting with the client was critical and lasted two hours due to the amount of information we had to cover. They had a lot of questions related to the budget assumptions, the test fit details, the financial analysis model, each landlord's motivations and interest level in their tenancy and, of course, which landlord might be willing to give the best deal! At the end of the meeting we concluded one of the relocation options was less attractive, but we agreed to send counterproposals to the other four options, which still included two options with our existing landlord.

- I crafted counterproposals, which were approved by the client prior to sending them to the landlords.

- Once the landlords responded with their second-round proposals, we updated our financial analysis and met again with the client.

- At this point it was abundantly clear that renovating the existing space and renegotiating the lease would be the most cost-effective option. It closely aligned with my client's Success Factors, and the client really didn't want to move anyway! But, of course, their landlord didn't know that. We presented an overview of the process to the co-founder, who approved the direction of the project and authorized us to prepare a Letter of Intent to send to the existing landlord.

- After several final rounds of negotiations, the Letter of Intent was signed, and the landlord drafted a lease amendment.
- We engaged a real estate attorney, and I worked with the attorney and the client to negotiate the amendment.

Let's take a quick break from the process and talk about how we structured the deal terms. My client extended the lease term for an additional seven years, seven months (from Aug. 1, 2018, through Feb. 28, 2026). In exchange for the extension, the landlord provided the following:

- A reduction of the rental rate by $4.00 PSF per year (an ongoing annual value of $80,000 per year).
- Seven months free rent (a value of $300,000).
- $600,000 ($30.00 PSF) tenant improvement allowance, two-thirds of which paid for construction upgrades and one-third of which could be converted to additional free rent.
- A new termination option effective July 31, 2023, with notice on July 31, 2022.

Why did the landlord provide such attractive terms? First of all, the market was slow and rental rates had declined since the last lease was structured in 2007, so my client's rent was above market for the building and surrounding buildings. Secondly, the tenant's termination penalty of three months' rent was so low that several landlords in the vicinity gladly would have written my client a check to pay the penalty and entice them to relocate to their building on Feb. 1, 2016.

We had other landlords lined up to move us into their buildings, and the existing landlord was forced to compete with two very threatening relocation options. Had the termination penalty been much higher, the existing landlord would not have considered it a real threat for my client to relocate, since the large penalty would likely make a relocation cost prohibitive.

## Design, Construction and Move-in: 6 months

As I write this book, we are in the middle of this final stage of the process. Here's what will happen:

- The architect's contract for design services will be reviewed and signed. Up until this point we only had a small contract in place for programming and test fit services.
- The project manager's contract will be revised and signed now that the exact scope of the project has been defined.
- The architect will have a visioning session with the client to discuss finer details of the design, finishes, furniture and cultural elements of the space. This is a two-hour meeting that is very hands on and heavily focused on helping the client identify creative elements of the business and culture that will impact the final design of the space.
- The project manager will continue to expand the team as the design process unfolds, including a mechanical, electrical and plumbing engineer (MEP), audio visual (AV) consultant and a furniture vendor.

- Once the test fits are further revised and approved, the architect will move into the schematic design phase. In this phase the architect takes what was learned from the visioning session and creates a conceptual design scheme with actual colors, sketches of elevations and scale.

- The architect then moves into a phase called design development, which will result in a final set of material finishes, 3-D modeling of particular areas of the space and final approval of the design direction. At this stage, the materials will be selected and the project manager will prepare a revised budget.

- The architect and MEP will prepare construction drawings that will be presented to the client for approval prior to issuing them to three general contractors (GCs) to be bid on. Sometimes a GC will be engaged earlier in the process based on their profit on the project. In that type of scenario, the GC would commit to a percentage profit on the project and then work with the client to get the best prices from various subcontractors. Other times (for example, in our scenario) a GC will bid on the project at this stage of the process and be awarded the project based on their bid. There are other details that we could discuss such as Lump Sum bidding vs. Cost Plus bidding, but I would just recommend that you ask your project manager or architect for their opinion on all of the above when you get to this stage in your process.

- After the construction drawings have been presented to the city for approval and a permit is issued, construction can begin.

Whew! I know that was a lot of information. This is as far

as I'll go for the purposes of this book. If you'd like more detail on the construction process, the pre-move process and move-in checklists (which can be very long!), please email me at **jon@kickingoffyourofficelease.com**, and I'll happily send you some examples.

As we wrap up this chapter on your Schedule, here is a summary of what to keep top of mind so you develop a thorough strategy and avoid costly mistakes.

- ☑ The most important message as it relates to a schedule is to start early. Like most projects in life, a leasing process typically takes longer than you'd anticipate, and I always encourage my clients to get the ball rolling as soon as possible. To put it another way: I've never had a client say, "Gosh, I wish I would have started this whole process a lot later!"

- ☑ Consistently ask that your architect and project manager provide up-to-date schedules and budgets as the process unfolds. You don't want to be surprised by any long lead-time items that will delay construction.

- ☑ Ask questions. Lots of questions. This process is very detailed, and there are many steps. Don't be afraid to inquire about what's around the corner.

- ☑ Get contracts with the architect, project manager and other vendors signed before the project starts to avoid miscommunication about what was expected of each team member.

- ☑ Give yourself a buffer on the schedule when you initially create it. You'll probably use it.

Let's move on to our final chapter on budgets, and then you're done!

# STEP 6

# *What Is Your Budget?*

*Calculating the estimated financial projections that factor into your budget prior to kicking off your leasing project.*

The last of your Kick-Off Questions also happens to be the most challenging to pinpoint and the most risky if not determined properly. The purpose of this chapter is to outline the high-level considerations related to budget and to familiarize you with what costs are included in an office leasing project. Please note that you also will need to have a conversation with a real estate advisor, architect or project manager to gain additional color for what's typical in your market to fully understand your potential budget.

## CURRENT LEASE COSTS

The first data point you need to be crystal clear on is what you are paying right now. To do this, you should review your lease and your most recent rent invoice. Factor in any other monthly costs that are not paid directly to the landlord (electricity, HVAC, janitorial, parking, to name a few). Most Class

A and B buildings will include HVAC and janitorial in the rent.

Electricity is often paid directly to the utility provider. Parking may or not be included in the lease. If you received any free rent as a part of your lease, confirm if it already has been applied.

Reviewing your lease and rent invoice will help you determine your lease costs on a cash basis. Ask your finance department for your GAAP rent, if applicable, and your depreciation schedules if you want to further understand your lease obligations.

Your rental rate is likely structured in one of two ways: Net (sometimes called Triple Net or NNN) or Gross. The rent section of your lease should state which one it is. You can also look at your rent invoice, and if the real estate taxes and operating expenses are very low, you probably have a gross lease.

## Net Lease

In a Net Lease, the tenant pays Net Rent, or "Base Rent," and then on top of that, the tenant's pro rata share of the building's Real Estate Taxes and Operating Expenses (T&O) for each calendar year. The industry term for paying T&O is often referred to as "Real Estate Taxes & Operating Expense passthroughs" because they are passed through the landlord directly to the tenant.

For example: If the landlord estimates that the T&O will be $12.00 per-square-foot (PSF) per year in 2015, they will invoice the tenant for $1.00 PSF per month ($12.00 PSF per year) and then true up any underpayment or overpayment in early 2016 once the landlord's accounting records are completed. Let's say the actual T&O for the 2015 calendar year is $12.60 PSF. The landlord will then invoice the tenant for an additional $0.60 PSF in early 2016. If the actual T&O is $11.90 PSF, the landlord will give the tenant a $0.10 PSF credit on the tenant's next rent statement.

## Gross Lease

In a Gross Lease, the tenant pays Gross Rent, which includes the T&O for the initial calendar year. The tenant will still pay its pro rata share of T&O, but only the increases in the T&O over the year that the tenant moves into the building. The year the tenant moves into the building is called the Base Year.

For example: Assume a tenant's Lease Commencement Date is Sep. 1, 2015, there was a 2015 Base Year and the T&O was $12.00 PSF in 2015. The tenant will not pay any T&O until Jan. 1, 2016. In 2016, if the T&O is estimated to increase to $12.60 PSF, the landlord will pass through an estimated $0.60 PSF in 2016 to the tenant ($0.05 PSF per month). Any underpayment or overpayment will be trued up in early 2017. This may seem like a lot of numbers to process, but these are concepts you must learn for basic office leasing literacy.

# FUTURE LEASE COSTS

The simplest way to think about your future budget is to separate the costs into two buckets: One-time Costs (sometimes called a capital expenditure or capex) and Ongoing Rent Costs.

## One-time Costs

As you prepare your One-time Costs, you will need estimates for the bullet point costs outlined below. Most professionals within the commercial real estate industry think in terms of price per-square-foot along with the actual dollar amount. Based on your most likely scenarios, you can ask a real estate advisor for high-level estimates for each of the factors below.

But be warned: Giving precise construction estimates

without having significant details on scope and finish quality is a real challenge. Your goal early on in the process is simply to understand the potential capex range of costs based on what you have spent on other similar projects and what other companies in your industry or in your market typically spend. High-level budget estimates can be valuable as you brainstorm conceptual scenarios prior to kicking off a project, but don't take them to the bank based on a two-minute conversation.

Here are the One-time Costs you should focus on:

- Hard costs (construction).
- Soft costs (professional fees).
  - » Architectural.
  - » Mechanical, electrical, plumbing (MEP) engineers.
  - » Project management.
  - » IT/Audio Visual (AV)/security consultant.
- Wiring and cabling.
- Furniture.
- Moving.
- AV.
- Decommissioning your current space (removing furniture, wiring or other required elements to deliver the space back to the landlord if you are relocating from your current space).
- Contingency: I recommend holding a contingency equal to 10 percent of all of the costs above at the beginning of the project, which can be decreased to 5 percent once budgets have been further defined.
- TI Allowance: What allowance is offered by the landlord to offset your One-time Costs?

One-time Costs will, of course, vary with different scenarios like renewing, relocating to space that has already been demolished (often called demo'd or raw space), relocating to a space with some existing conditions, the impact of building location or quality, etc. There are other costs to keep in mind, such as updating stationery or marketing materials, if required. The loss of productivity associated with a major renovation or relocation will also be significant and should be taken into account, although it is quite difficult to allocate an estimated cost to that loss in time.

Another caveat: Most real estate advisors will NOT carry other IT costs in their budgets—new phones, server racks or computer equipment, for example. Other monthly IT costs like Internet, phone or cable aren't typically carried in a real estate advisor's budget either. As I mentioned in the Internal Team section from Step Four, those are budgets that you should create with input from your own IT department and your IT service partners.

## Ongoing Costs

Your Ongoing Costs will include:

- Base Rent (confirm if Net or Gross, based on your market and the buildings you would consider).
- Real Estate Taxes and Operating Expenses (T&O). Confirm if Net or Gross.
- Free rent (confirm in which months it is offered and if it applies to the Base Rent, T&O or both. Free rent that only applies to the Net Rent is called Net Free Rent and free rent that also abates the T&O is called Gross Free Rent).
- Electricity (if not included in the Base Rent, or if re-

quired after normal business hours).
- HVAC (if not included in the Base Rent, or if required after normal business hours).
- Janitorial (if not included in the Base Rent).
- Parking (if not included in the Base Rent).

When estimating Ongoing Costs, common practice is to include any fixed rent payments and escalations as explicitly stated in the lease ($0.50 PSF per year, 3 percent per year, whatever is agreed to in the lease or customary in the market). For all other ongoing cost estimates that are not explicitly stated in the lease, a standard practice is to escalate the estimates by 3 percent per year (T&O, ongoing electricity costs, HVAC, or janitorial, for example).

From a market perspective, you'll want to think through a few variables that will impact your budget:

- What class building are you currently located in?
- What's the market rent for your building today, and how does that compare to what you are currently paying?
- What's the market rent for comparable buildings of similar quality?
- What's the market rent for a different class of building if you choose to upgrade or downgrade?
- What's the market rent for a different submarket or building location?
- What's the market rent for the most expensive buildings (Class A) and the least expensive (Class C)?

To make this more practical, let me tell you about the budgets we just presented to a growing law firm client who asked me many of the questions above. They were in a very old space and wanted to move to a new 100,000 square foot space and build it out from scratch.

One-time Costs (PSF costs to be multiplied by 100,000 square feet):

- Hard costs (construction): $120.00 PSF.
- Soft costs (professional fees): $10.00 PSF.
- Wiring and Cabling: $4.00 PSF.
- Furniture: $30.00 PSF.
- Moving: $1.50 PSF.
- AV: $5.00 PSF.
- Decommissioning the former space: $1.00 PSF.
- Contingency: 10 percent of the total costs: $17.15 PSF.
- **Total Costs of $188.65 PSF**.
- The landlord would provide a TI Allowance of $70.00 PSF, which leaves the tenant with estimated One-time Costs of $118.65 PSF or $11.87 million.

Ongoing Costs (Annual PSF costs to be multiplied by 100,000 square feet):

- Base Rent: $25.00 PSF Net with $0.50 PSF annual escalations.
- Real Estate Taxes and Operating Expenses (T&O): 2016 estimates of $17.00 PSF, escalating at 3 percent per year.
- Free rent: 12 months Gross Free Rent ($42.00 PSF).
- Electricity: $1.25 PSF paid directly to the local utility provider, escalating at 3 percent per year.
- HVAC: Included in Base Net Rent.
- Janitorial: Included in Base Net Rent.
- Parking: $250 per space per month, assuming five

spaces in the lease, escalating at 3 percent per year.

If you would like me to send you a sample financial analysis model in Excel which incorporates One-time Costs and Ongoing Costs, please feel free to email me at **jon@kickingoffyourofficelease.com**.

As we wrap up this chapter on your Budget, here is a summary of what to keep top of mind so you develop a thorough strategy and avoid costly mistakes.

☑ As with all budgets, stay conservative. If you think you want to be in a Class B building, use Base Rent estimates for Class A- buildings. If you think you'll spend (x) amount on hard costs to build new space, include (x) plus 10 percent for now. You don't want to get approval on a budget and then have to go back again to increase it!

☑ If you know that building out new space from scratch will cost you more than you want to spend, even after deducting the TI Allowance offered by the landlord, and you have no capex budget to work with, don't waste your time by focusing on scenarios that require that type of financial commitment.

☑ Make sure that you understand the Net vs. Gross Rent structure and what a building's T&O projections are, especially in new buildings or buildings that are being redeveloped. Unfortunately it's far too common that tenants sign leases without knowing what future exposure they are committing to.

☑ Finding existing condition (second-generation space) or subleases can be a great way to save on One-time Costs and Ongoing Costs, but there are a myriad of other hassles and factors associated with being a subtenant. Ask your advisors if a sublease is the right scenario for you.

# Kicking Off Your Office Lease

Real estate, whether in a home or an office, is personal. It's emotional. It causes disagreements and arguments, and potential changes to someone's space will bring out all sorts of reactions. Tell someone they have to drive 10 more minutes to work or that you're changing their office size or that you're getting a new fridge for their lunch, and watch Pandora's Box fly open! The risk associated with a poorly managed office lease relocation or renewal is massive. A successful project, on the other hand, can change the future course of a company and send your own career on a new trajectory.

Well, guess what: You're ready to get started on the right track!

The goal of this book has been to equip you with enough information in a short time so that you feel confident writing an email to your team that says, "OK, folks, it's time to get our office lease process started. Let's all meet to brainstorm how to kick this off. I've got my thoughts organized, and I'm really looking forward to getting yours as well."

When you walk into that meeting, you'll now be armed with the tools, concepts and familiarity of the process to confidently lead the discussion and walk away with a clear, concise vision for your upcoming project. You've thought through your Deficiency Drivers, Success Factors, Scenarios, Team, Schedule and Budget, and how they all apply to your specific situation. On that basis, I'll simply conclude with a few reminders as you prepare for that first meeting:

- Carefully think through who you want in that room. Remember: This conversation is meant to be high-level and strategic.

- Come prepared with an understanding of how much space you have, the lease expiration and what you're paying per-square-foot, per month and per year.

- Have a conversation with a real estate advisor prior to the meeting so that you have a firm grasp of what's happening in the office leasing market—specifically in your building and the surrounding area (vacancy rate, rental rates, recently completed deals, how your rent compares to the market and other market-related questions I outlined in the previous chapter).

- Use the six Kick-Off Questions to lead the discussion and engage the room to understand everyone's Deficiency Drivers, Success Factors and perceived Scenarios.

- Get consensus around the three real estate advisors who you plan on interviewing. If you don't have three good companies to interview, discuss how you'll identify them.

- Ask about any other previous relationships that your company has with architects, project managers or general contractors.

- At the end of the meeting, your next steps should include:
  » A plan to secure whatever approvals are required to kick off your process (this may not be necessary if your company has a more flat leadership structure).

» A plan to set up interviews with the three real estate advisors.

As we have discussed, the real estate advisor is the quarterback of this entire process. Choose that advisor wisely! The stakes are high, not only for the project's success, but also for the ongoing success of your career development.

If you have any questions about anything, I'm happy to be a resource for you. Feel free to email me anytime at **jon@kickingoffyourofficelease.com** or visit my website at **www.kickingoffyourofficelease.com**.

To your success!

– Jon

# APPENDIX

# *Glossary of Terms*

*Many of these terms appear in the text of this book, but I've also included several others you'll encounter throughout your office leasing process.*

### Add-on Factor

Sometimes referred to as a Loss Factor, this is a factor or percentage that is applied to the Usable Square Footage to arrive at the Rentable Square Footage. It represents the common areas within a building that the tenant does not have exclusive use of, but are paid for by each tenant (building lobbies, columns, elevators, mechanical rooms, common corridors, bathrooms, etc.). Older buildings with many columns and large corridors typically have a larger Add-on Factor than newer buildings that are virtually column-free with more efficient floor plates.

### Audio Visual (AV)

Considered part of the IT budget, this includes items such as TVs or projectors, video conferencing equipment, speakers or microphones and other related equipment.

## Base Year

Used in a Gross Lease to calculate the increase in a tenant's Proportionate Share of Real Estate Taxes and Operating Expenses. The Base Year is typically the year that the tenant moves into the building. For example, if the Real Estate Taxes and Operating Expenses increase in year two, the tenant only pays the difference between the year two expenses and the year one (Base Year) expenses.

## Benching Work Stations

Work stations that only have one horizontal work surface as opposed to larger 6-by-6 or 8-by-8 foot work stations that have both a horizontal and a perpendicular/side work surface. Benching Work Stations are smaller and more efficient, although they have less storage and potentially less privacy than traditional two-sided work stations.

## Building Class

Classified as A, B or C, depending on the building's age, infrastructure (HVAC, elevators, power, data, telecommunications connectivity), amenities, tenants, location, and other factors. Building Class can be relative and classified on a market-to-market basis. The plus (+) or minus (-) sign may be used to further categorize a building, for example B+ or A-.

## Capital Expenditure (Capex)

A One-time Cost incurred during the construction process. When accounted for on a cash basis, Capex is incurred in the year in which the dollars are spent. When accounted for on an accrual/GAAP basis, Capex is spread over the life of the lease term or the appropriate accounting schedule.

## Deficiency Drivers

Challenges within a space, lease, building, location or otherwise that are not ideal for a tenant. Clearly understanding your Deficiency Drivers leads to greater clarity on potential solutions for the deficiencies. See *Success Factors.*

## Depreciation

The decreasing value of an asset over the life of the lease term, or over the useful life of the asset (i.e. furniture or technology will depreciate at a different schedule than Hard Cost construction improvements).

## Escalation

The increase of Rent which typically takes place every year or across another consistent time frame (i.e. every three or five years). Escalations can take the form of a percentage or fixed increase ($0.50 per rentable square foot per year, $1.00 per rentable square foot per year, etc.).

## Free-Addressing

The use of shared desks for particular departments or an entire office whereas an employee does not have a dedicated seat. Sometimes called "hoteling" or "hot-desking."

## Free Rent

Typically applied in the form of a certain number of months free. Net Free Rent means the tenant does not need to pay the Net Rent, but still pays Real Estate Taxes and Operating Expenses. Gross Free Rent means the tenant does not have to pay anything, even the Real Estate Taxes and Operating Expenses.

## Gross Lease

In a Gross Lease, the tenant pays the Gross Rent as outlined in the lease, plus the tenant's Proportionate Share of the increase in Real Estate Taxes and Operating Expenses over and above the Base Year. See *Net Lease.*

## Gross Rent

Sometimes called "Modified Gross," this is the Net Rent plus the Real Estate Taxes and Operating Expenses combined. See *Net Rent.*

## Hard Costs

Construction costs built into the physical space: drywall, ceilings, HVAC systems, flooring, carpet, electrical, glass, telecom/data wiring, lighting, millwork and other non-removable items. See *Soft Costs.*

## Heating, Ventilation, Air Conditioning (HVAC)

Sometimes provided on a monthly basis by the landlord as a part of the Operating Expenses, and sometimes paid for by the tenant. If provided by the landlord, normal business hours are typically 8 a.m. to 6 p.m. from Monday to Friday and 8 a.m. to 1 p.m. on Saturdays, but subject to vary based on the building and the market.

## Lease

The legal, binding document used to outline the responsibilities of a tenant and a landlord.

## Letter of Credit (LOC)

A financial instrument used in place of a cash security deposit whereas the tenant sets aside a certain amount of money with the tenant's bank so that, in the case of a tenant default, the landlord can draw down on the LOC as if it were the landlord's own asset. Landlords prefer to have an LOC as opposed to a cash security deposit because in bankruptcy an LOC may be drawn down on immediately, whereas a cash security deposit might have to be offered up as an asset of the tenant and subject to other creditors. There is typically a 1 percent annual LOC processing fee, paid for by the tenant, but this is offset by any interest received by the tenant.

## Letter of Intent (LOI)

Sometimes called a "Term Sheet," the LOI is a summary of deal terms that are mutually agreed upon by the tenant and the landlord. The LOI is then used by attorneys to draft the lease document. Most LOIs are not legally binding.

## Mechanical, Electrical, and Plumbing (MEP)

The drawings prepared by an MEP engineer in conjunction with architectural construction plans.

## Net Lease

In a Net Lease, the tenant pays the Net Rent as outlined in the lease, plus the tenant's actual Proportionate Share of Real Estate Taxes and Operating Expenses for the entire building. See *Gross Lease.*

## Net Rent

Sometimes called "Base Rent", "Net" or "NNN", Net Rent does not include the Real Estate Taxes or Operating Expenses and typically refers to the Base Rent as stated in the lease. Often stated on a per-square-foot, monthly and annual basis. See *Gross Rent.*

## Operating Expenses (Opex)

Sometimes called "Common Area Maintenance" (CAM), these are the costs required to run the building. In a Net Lease, the tenant pays their proportionate share each year, which can increase or decrease based on the actual Operating Expenses. In a Gross Lease, the tenant only pays the increase in Operating Expenses over the Base Year. Each building and market are different, but typical operating expenses will include some or all of the following: HVAC, gas, water, electricity, security, cleaning and janitorial, management/administrative fees, repairs and maintenance and insurance.

## Per-Square-Foot (PSF)

A term used to calculate the allocation of rent, Tenant Improvement Allowance or other costs based on the size of a tenant's rentable square footage within a building.

## Program

Sometimes called a "Space Program," this document created by an architect summarizes the space planning needs of a business (i.e. the number and size of offices, work stations, conference rooms, etc.) and the corresponding estimated square footage requirement to satisfy each need. When totaled, the final Program estimates the total Usable and Rentable Square Footage for the project. Architects use the Program as a road map to create Test Fits.

## Project Manager

A consultant who manages the construction process, most importantly the budget and the schedule. All external project team members report to the Project Manager (architect, general contractor, AV consultants, MEP engineers, move vendors, furniture vendors, telecom/data vendors, phone vendors, security consultants, signage vendors, etc.). Project Managers are typically engaged on larger projects or smaller projects with high construction costs.

## Proportionate Share

The percentage of the building that a tenant occupies. Used by landlords to calculate the distribution of costs across the different tenants in a building.

## Real Estate Taxes (Tax)

The property taxes paid by a landlord that are passed through to tenants. In a Net Lease, the tenant pays their Proportionate Share each year, which can increase or decrease based on the actual Real Estate Taxes. In a Gross Lease, the tenant only pays the increase in Real Estate Taxes over the Base Year.

## Request for Proposal (RFP)

Used for interviewing External Team Members and also used when soliciting proposals from buildings.

## Rentable Square Feet (RSF)

The square footage on which a tenant pays rent. It is calculated by multiplying the Usable Square Footage by an Add-on Factor or Loss Factor. The RSF incorporates every square foot of the building allocated to tenants based on each tenant's Proportionate Share, including the common areas that are not exclusive to the tenant.

## Security Deposit

Determined based on a tenant's financials and delivered by the tenant to the landlord when a Lease is signed in the form of a cash deposit or a Letter of Credit. Some Security Deposits have a burn down or reduction schedule throughout the life of the lease, whereby the Security Deposit decreases per a mutually agreed upon schedule.

## Soft Costs

Non-construction costs that are required during a construction project: architectural fees, MEP fees, project management, IT or other consulting fees. See *Hard Costs.*

## Success Factors

The big-picture goals of the project that drive the decision making process. See *Deficiency Drivers.*

## Success Factor Weighted Matrix

A tool used to organize, prioritize and measure the key Success Factors of a project. The goal of the matrix is to create consensus with key stakeholders for various building or scenario alternatives.

## Tenant Improvement Allowance (TI Allowance or TI)

A cash allowance provided by a landlord to prepare a space for a tenant's occupancy. Most TI Allowances have stipulations as to how much needs to be spent on Hard Costs, Soft Costs or other costs. Typically stated on a PSF basis (i.e. $10.00 PSF), or a cash number (i.e. $100,000).

## Test Fit

A 2-D floor plan prepared by an architect to confirm if the tenant's Program requirements can be accommodated within a particular space under consideration. In some markets, a landlord might reimburse the tenant's architect for an initial Test Fit plus one revision of the Test Fit. For Turnkey Construction projects, the landlord typically uses their own in-house architect or their preferred third party architect to prepare a Test Fit.

## Turnkey Construction
A term used if the landlord manages the construction per a mutually agreed upon space plan or within a certain Tenant Improvement Allowance cap. If the landlord does not manage the construction, the landlord provides a Tenant Improvement Allowance to the tenant and the tenant manages the construction.

## Usable Square Feet (USF)
The floor area within a tenant's space that is usable by the tenant exclusively. Architects focus on the USF because it outlines the area within which they can plan and design the actual space. See *Rentable Square Feet.*

## White Noise
An overhead sound system installed in offices to manage sound levels, particularly in open office environments.

## Workplace Strategy
A consulting approach that analyzes how a company uses office space, specifically in light of the impact that technology is making on the workplace. Many real estate services firms and architectural firms have a dedicated Workplace Strategy consulting practice that consults with a tenant prior to actively engaging an architect.

# NOTES

# NOTES

# NOTES

NOTES

# NOTES

# NOTES

Made in the USA
Middletown, DE
06 February 2017